RECORDED VERSIONS GUITAR

AUTHENTIC TRANSCRIPTIONS
WITH NOTES AND TABLATURE

Transcribed by JESSE GRESS

THE BEATLES ABBEY ROAD

MW00848668

ISBN 0-7935-2303-6

Hal Leonard Publishing Corporation

7777 West Bluemound Road P.O. Box 13819 Milwaukee, WI 53213

Come Together

Words and Music by John Lennon and Paul McCartney

Moderately Slow Rock ♩ = 84
Intro

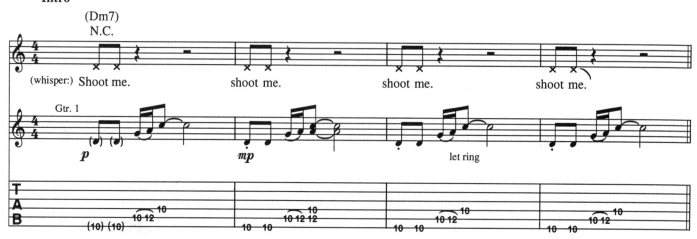

1st Verse

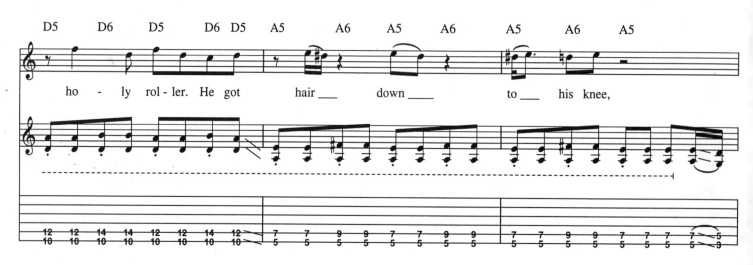

MCA music publishing

Guitar Solo

* Gtrs. 2, 3 use neck pickup w/ treble rolled off.

Something

By George Harrison

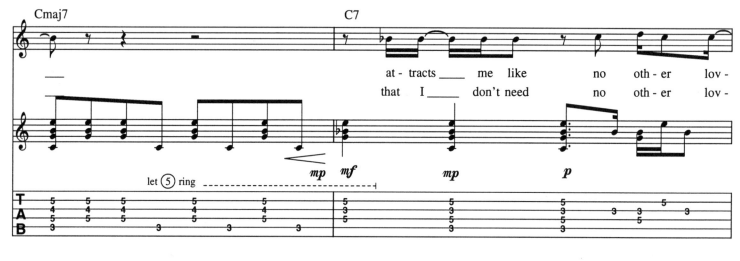

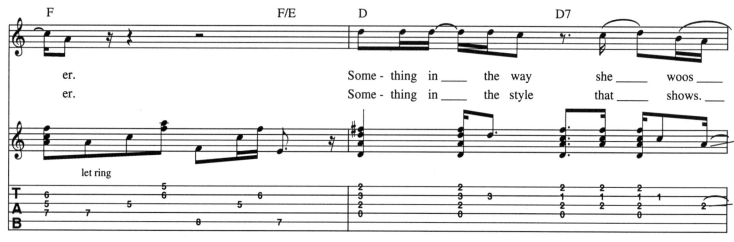

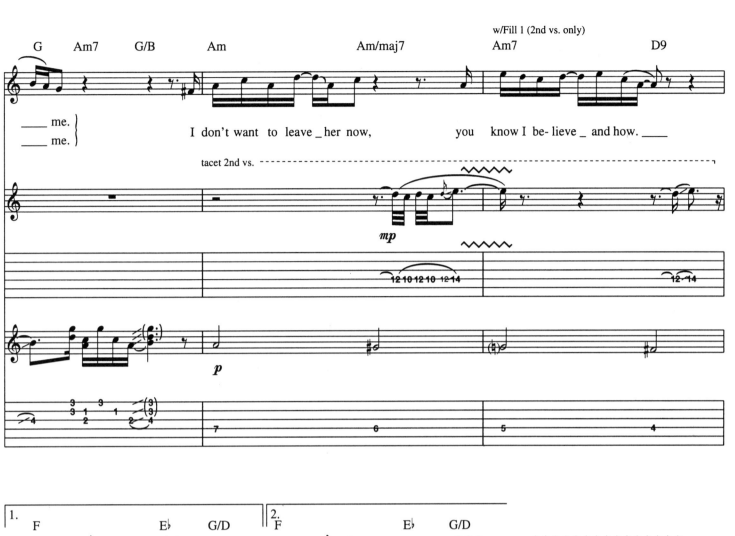

I don't want to leave _ her now,   you   know I be- lieve _ and how. ____

tacet 2nd vs.

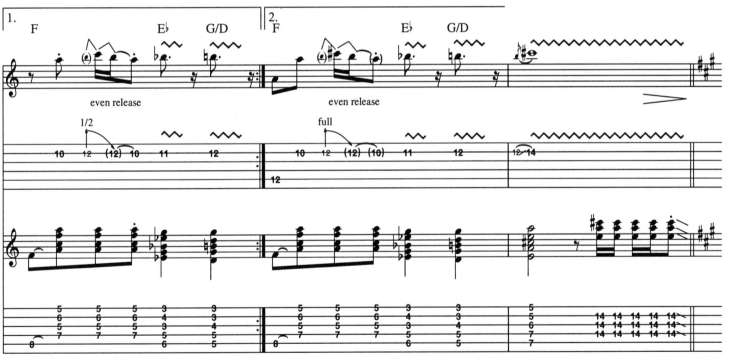

even release

even release

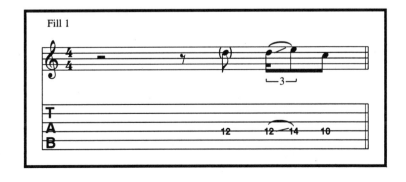

Fill 1

Bridge

You're ask-ing me _ will my _ love grow. I don't know, _____ I _____ don't _

strings arr. for gtr.

⑥ = D

even gliss

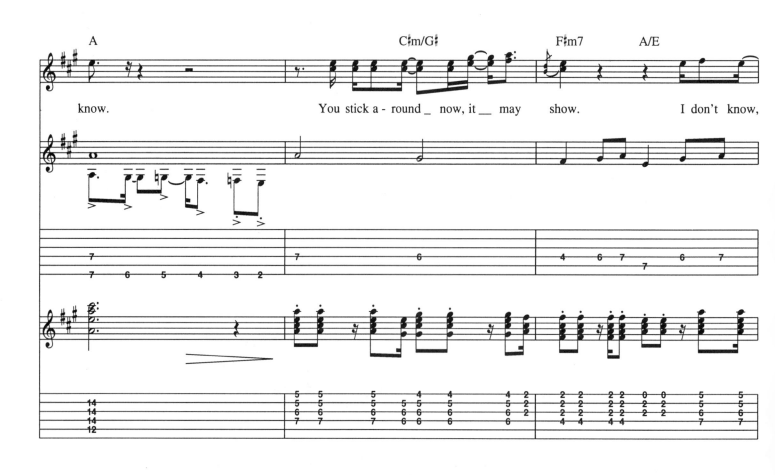

know. You stick a-round _ now, it _ may show. I don't know,

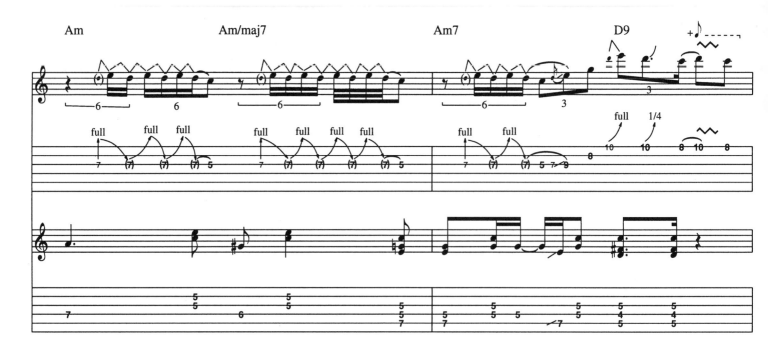

3rd Verse

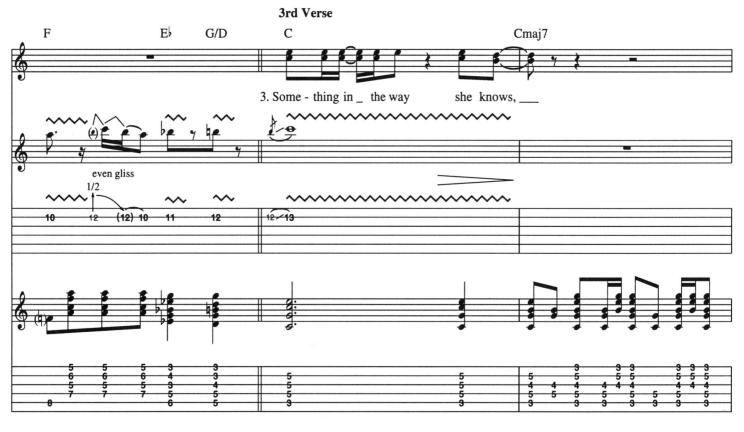

3. Some - thing in _ the way she knows, ___

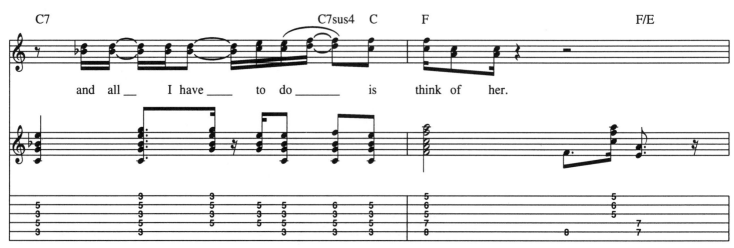

and all _ I have ___ to do _____ is think of her.

Some-thing in _ the things _ she _ shows _ me.   I don't want to leave _ her now,   you

know I be-lieve _ and how. _____

Maxwell's Silver Hammer

Words and Music by John Lennon and Paul McCartney

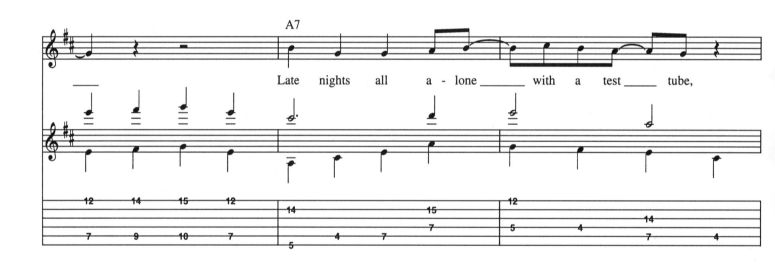

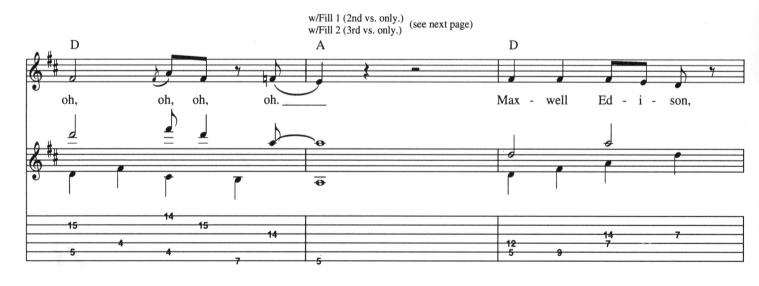

MCA music publishing

1.
Interlude
Em7 A7 D N.C. D F♯7
sure that she was dead.
Synth. arr. for gtr.
1/2
Bm D7 G D5/A G/B A/C♯ D A7 D
2.
Guitar solo
Em7 A7 D
sure that she was dead.
1/2
mf

Do - doot - do do   do.

Piano arr. for 2 gtrs.

Divisi

Acous. gtr. tacet

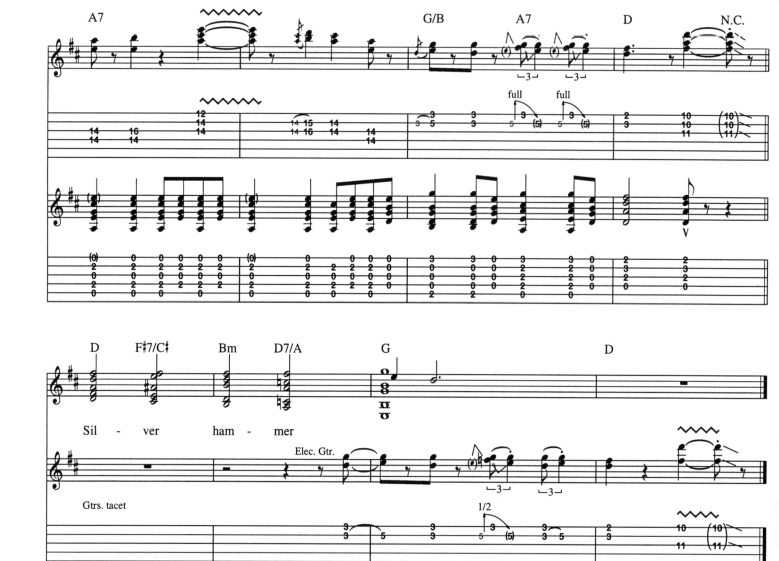

Additional lyrics:

2. Back in school again, Maxwell played the fool again,
   Teacher got annoyed.
   Wishing to avoid an unpleasant sce-e-e-ene.
   She tells Max to stay when the class has gone away,
   So he waits behind.
   Writing fifty times "I must not be so-o-o-o-o."
   But when she turns her back on the boy,
   He creeps up from behind.

Chorus: Bang! Bang1 Maxwell's silver hammer came down upon her head.
   Clang! Clang! Maxwell's silver hammer made sure that she was dead.

3. P.C. Thirty-one said, "We've caught a dirty one,"
   Maxwell stands alone.
   Painting testimonial pictures, oh, oh, oh, oh.
   Rose and Valerie screaming from the gallery
   Say he must go free (Maxwell must go free.)
   The judge does not agree and he tells them so-o-o-o.
   But as the words are leaving his lips,
   A noise comes from behind.

Chorus: Bang! Bang1 Maxwell's silver hammer came down upon his head.
   Clang! Clang! Maxwell's silver hammer made sure that he was dead, whoa, whoa, whoa.

Oh! Darling

Words and Music by John Lennon and Paul McCartney

MCA music publishing

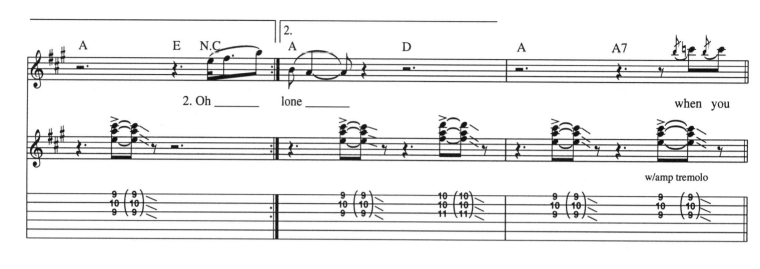

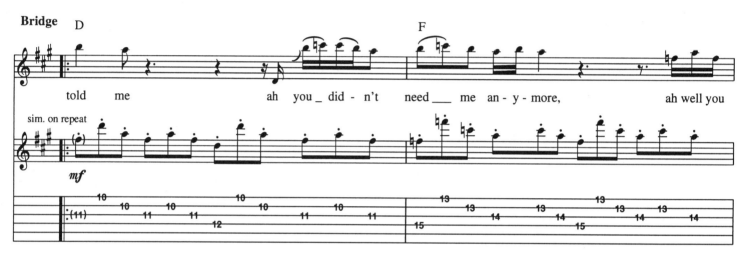

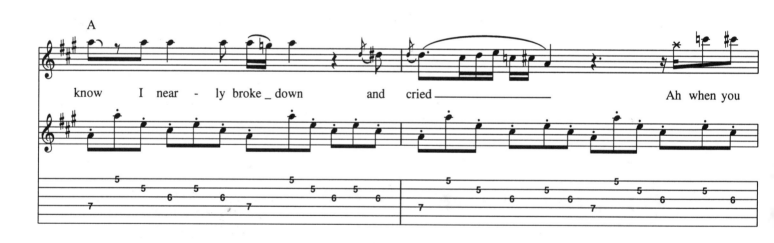

Octopus's Garden

Words and Music by Richard Starkey

Moderately Fast ♩ = 184
Intro

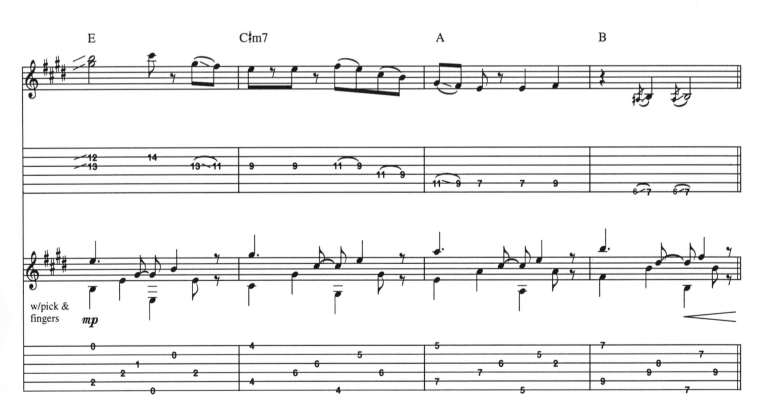

Today's Deals   Gift Cards   Help

Save now on Valentine's Day gifts

Shop by Department   **Search** Books

Go

Hello. **Sign in**
Your Account

0
Cart

Wish
List

Books   Advanced Search   Browse Subjects   New Releases   Best Sellers   The New York Times® Best Sellers   Children's Books   Textbooks   Sell Your Books

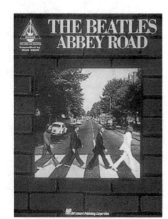

See larger image

Share your own customer images

Publisher: learn how customers can search inside this book.

Tell the Publisher!
I'd like to read this book on Kindle

Don't have a Kindle? Get your Kindle here, or download a **FREE** Kindle Reading App.

The Beatles - Abbey Road (Guitar Recorded Versions) [Paperback]

The Beatles (Author)

(3 customer reviews) |

(0)

Price: **$19.95** & eligible for **FREE Super Saver Shipping** on orders over $25. Details

In Stock.
Ships from and sold by **Amazon.com**. Gift-wrap available.

Only 12 left in stock--order soon (more on the way).

Want it delivered Tuesday, February 7? Order it in the next 21 hours and 43 minutes, and choose **One-Day Shipping** at checkout. Details

19 new from $11.99   20 used from $12.48
1 collectible from $17.99

Quantity: 1 ▾

or

Sign in to turn on 1-Click ordering.

or

Add to Cart with
FREE Two-Day Shipping

Amazon Prime Free Trial required. Sign up when you check out. Learn More

Sell Back Your Copy
For a **$1.20** Gift Card

Trade in ◉

Learn more

More Buying Choices

40 used & new from $11.99

Have one to sell?

Share

Book Description

Publication Date: **August 1, 1993** | Series: **Guitar Recorded Versions**

Matching folio to the classic album, including the songs: Come Together * Here Comes the Sun * Octopus's Garden * Something * and more.

Customers Viewing This Page May Be Interested in These Sponsored Links (What's this?)

Beatles Guitar Tab Books 🗗   Learn the songs of **the Beatles** with **guitar** tab books at Music Dispatch
www.musicdispatch.com

Beatles Abbey Road 🗗   View **Beatles Abbey Road**; Get Answers Now on Ask.com!
www.ask.com/**Beatles+Abbey+Road**

See a problem with these advertisements? Let us know

Advertise on Amazon

Frequently Bought Together

  +   +

Price For All Three: $59.85

Show availability and shipping details

☑ **This item:** The Beatles - Abbey Road (Guitar Recorded Versions) by The Beatles   Paperback $19.95
☑ The Beatles - Revolver (Guitar Recorded Version) by The Beatles   Paperback $19.95
☑ The Beatles - Sgt. Pepper's Lonely Hearts Club Band (Guitar Recorded Version) by The Beatles   Paperback $19.95

Customers Who Viewed This Item Also Bought

Page 1 of 6

Pre - Chorus

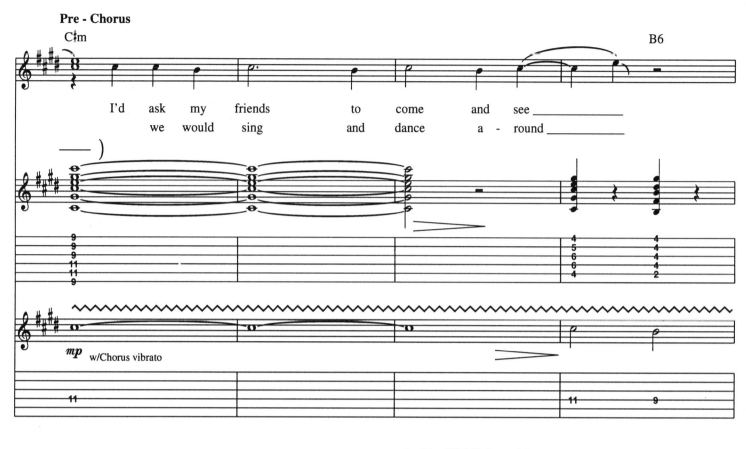

I'd   ask   my   friends   to   come   and   see _____

we   would   sing   and   dance   a - round _____

mp w/Chorus vibrato

* w/Rhy. Fill 1 (2nd vs. only)

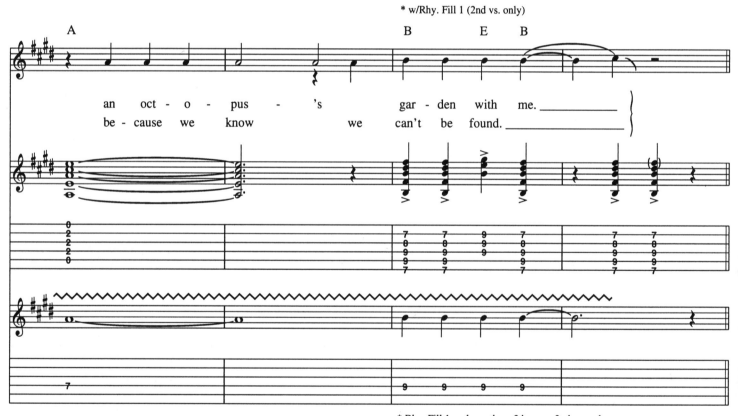

an   oct - o - pus - 's   gar - den   with   me. _____

be - cause   we   know   we   can't   be   found. _____

* Rhy. Fill 1 replaces these 2 bars on 2nd vs. only

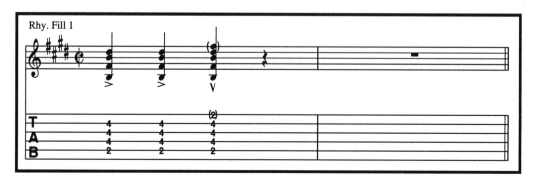

Rhy. Fill 1

30

Guitar Solo

knowing __ they're hap-py and they're safe..

(Hap - py and they're

we would be so hap-py you and me, ____

safe.)

Gtr. 3

mp

w/chorus vibrato

* Bass gtr. plays B

no one there to tell us what to do. ____

I Want You (She's So Heavy)

Words and Music by John Lennon and Paul McCartney

Tempo 1 Slow and heavy ♩. = 54

Intro

* w/bridge pick up

Tempo 2 ♩ = 115　　**1st Verse**

MCA music publishing

* played by organ throughout.

2nd Verse

you. _____ I want you so ____ bad, _____ babe

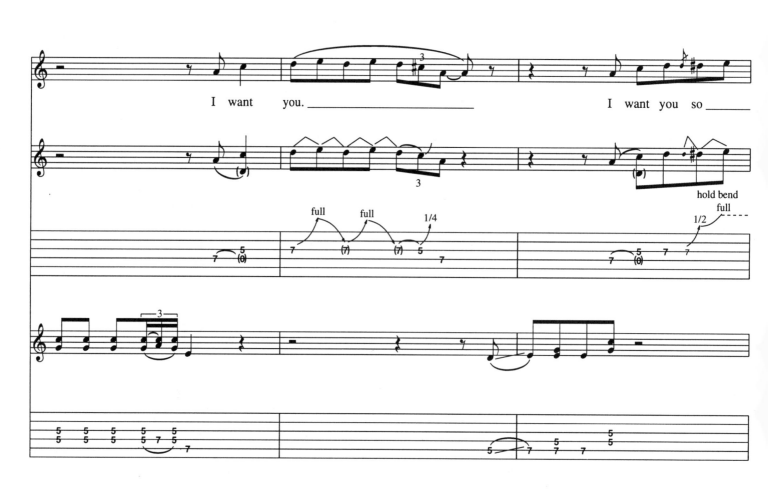

I want you. _____ I want you so _____

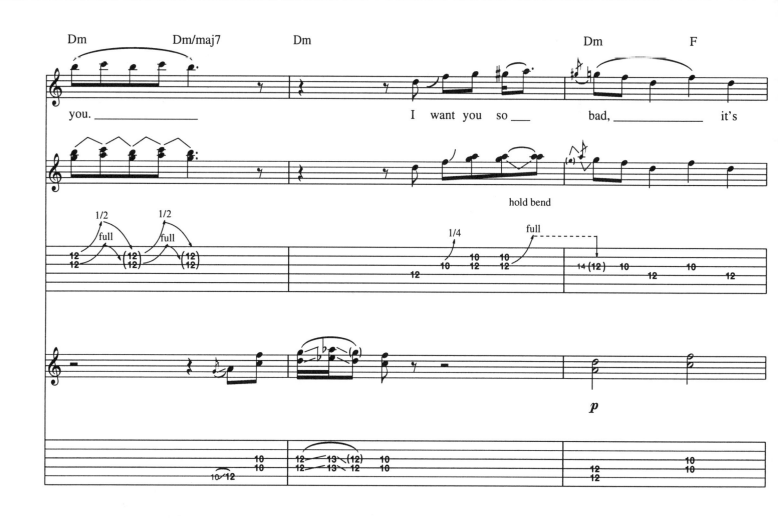

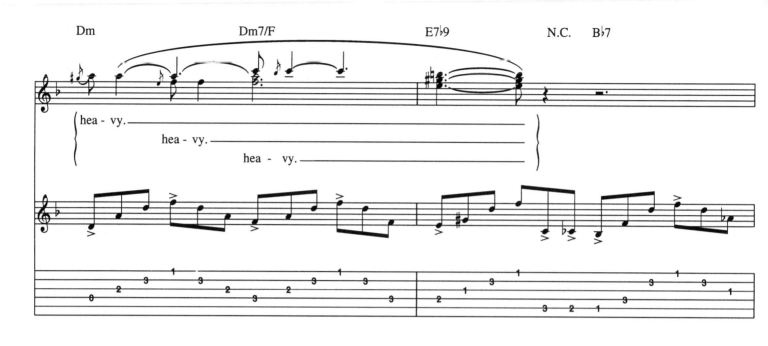

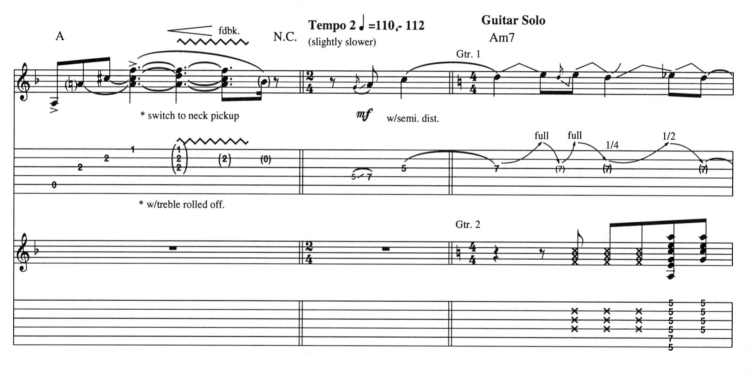

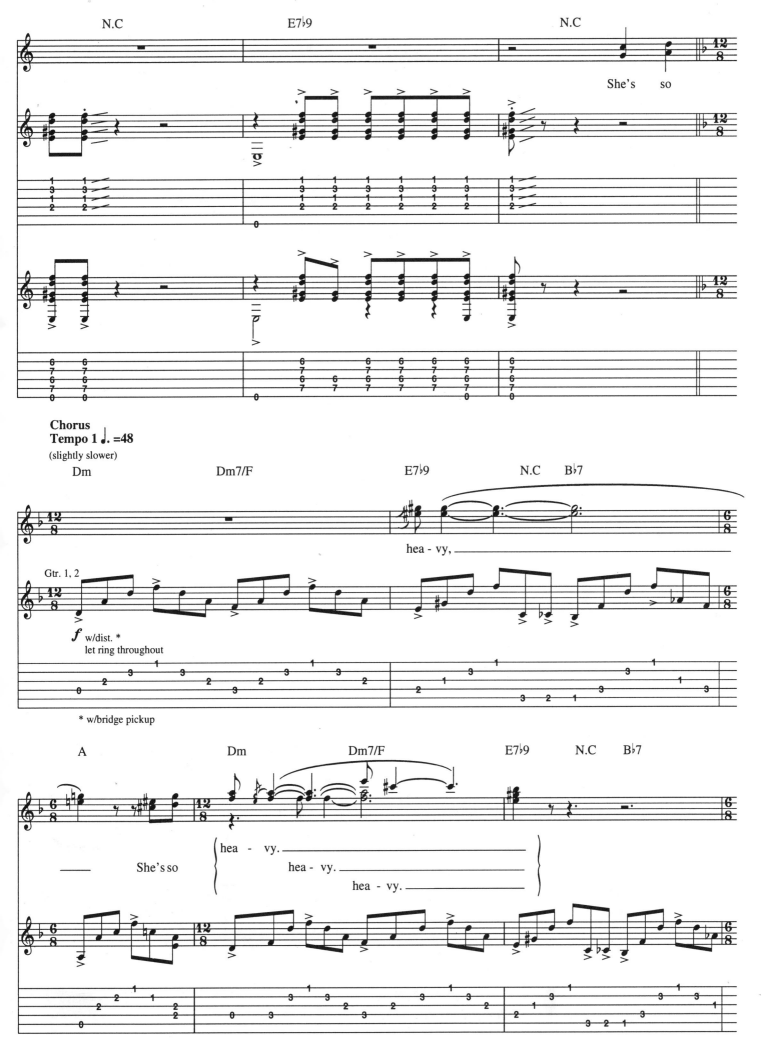

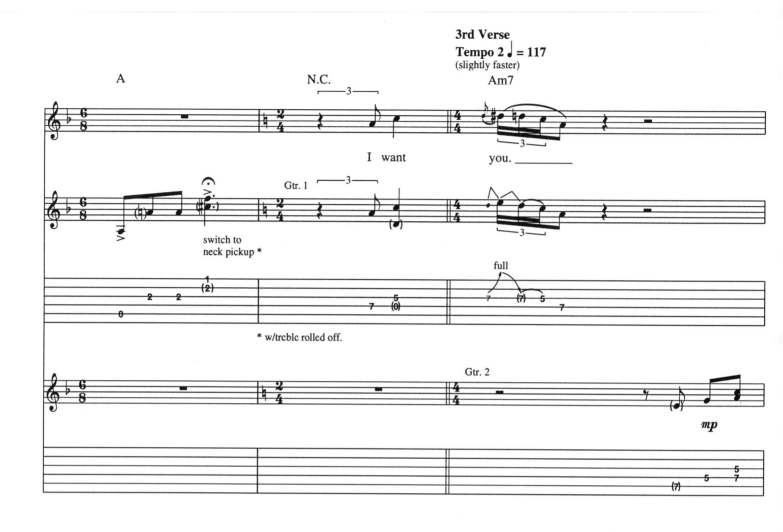

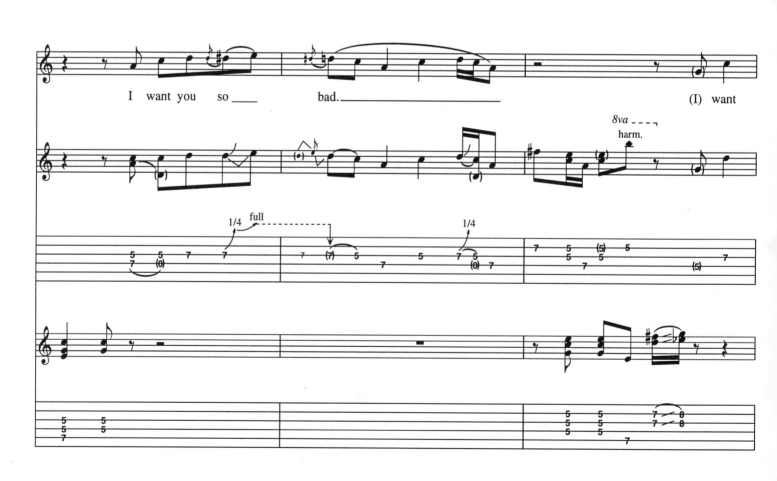

Chorus
Tempo 1 ♩. = 48
(slightly slower)

She's so

Here Comes The Sun

By George Harrison

2nd Verse

2. Lit- tle dar- lin', the smiles _____ re- turn - ing to ___ their fac - es.

Lit- tle dar- lin', it __ seems__ like _ years __ since you've _ been _ here. ___

𝄋 Chorus

Here comes _ the sun. ____ (Doo 'n' doo doo) Here comes _ the sun _____ 'n' I ___ say

it's al - right.

let ring

Because

Words and Music by John Lennon and Paul McCartney

MCA music publishing

You Never Give Me Your Money

Words and Music by
John Lennon and Paul McCartney

MCA music publishing

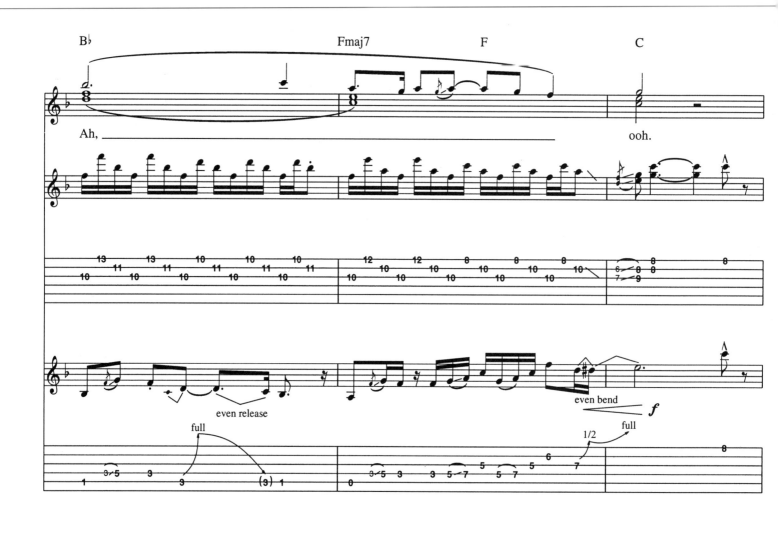

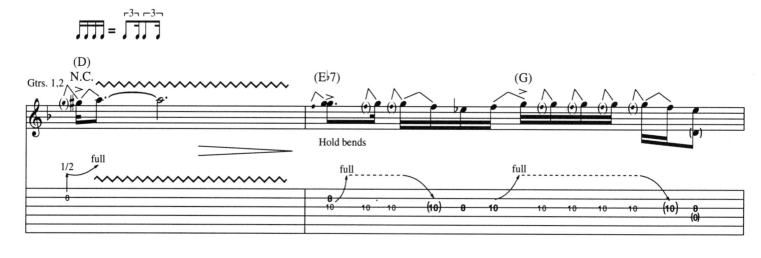

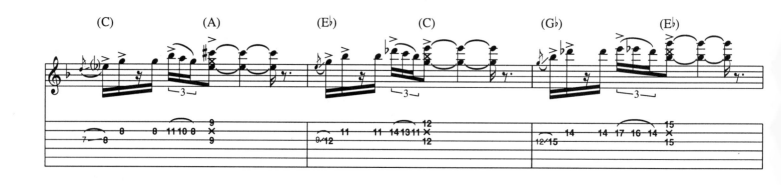

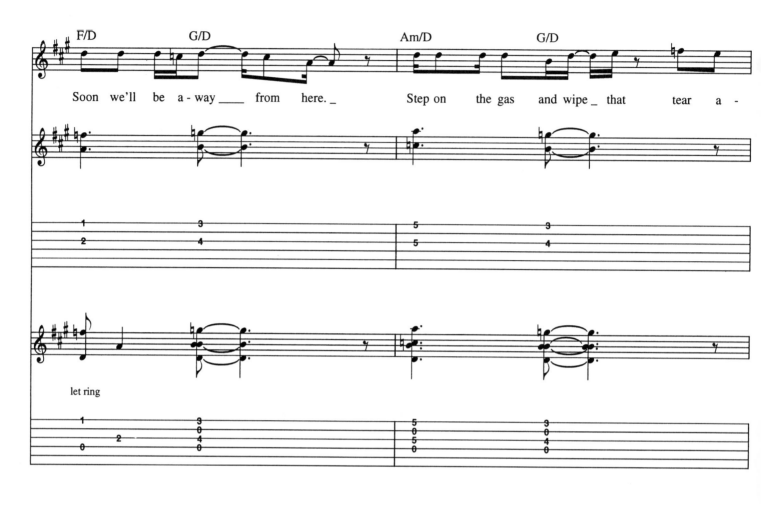

Soon we'll be a - way ____ from here. _ Step on the gas and wipe _ that tear a -

let ring

way. One sweet dream came _ true _____ to - day. __

semi.-P.M.

let ring throughout

let ring

1/2

Sun King

Words and Music by John Lennon and Paul McCartney

MCA music publishing

mor - e__ de fe - li - ce__ car - a fon.

let ring

dim.

Mun - do__ pa - pa - raz - zi__ mi a - mor - e__ chick - a fer - dy__ pa - ra - sol.

let ring

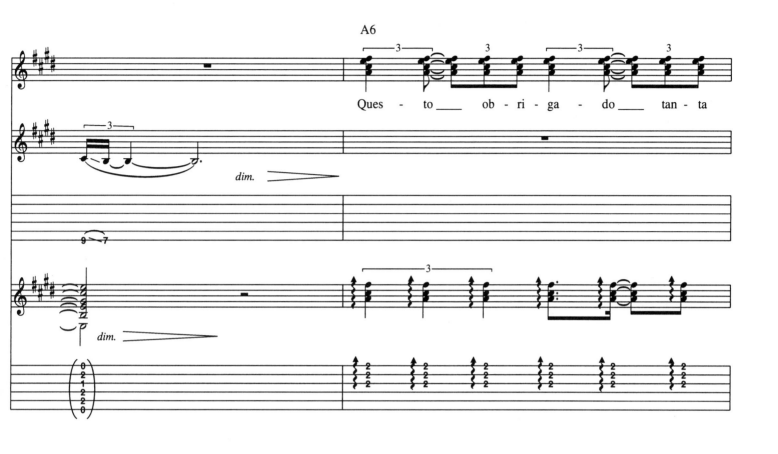

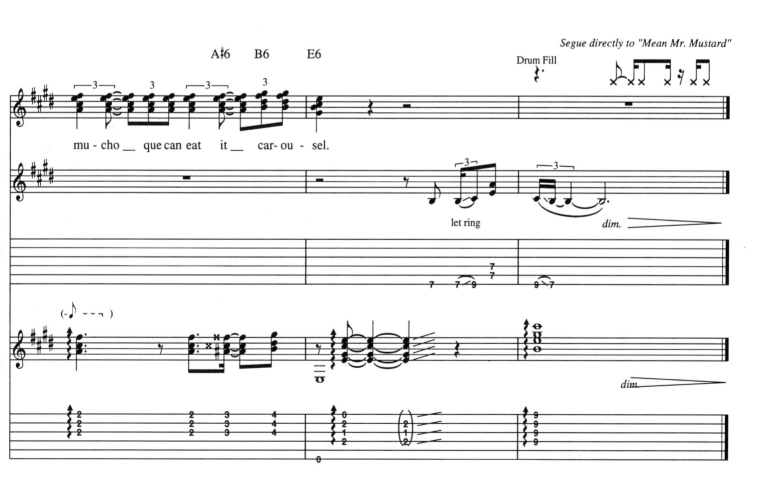

Mean Mr. Mustard

Words and Music by
John Lennon and Paul McCartney

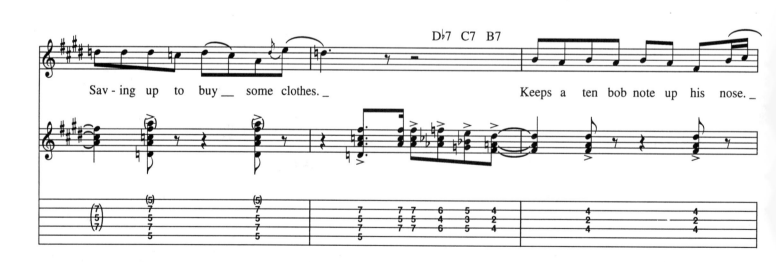

MCA music publishing

Polythene Pam

Words and Music by
John Lennon and Paul McCartney

see __ Pol - y - thene Pam.   Yeah,   yeah,   yeah. __

2. Get a dose of her in jack- boots and kilts. __

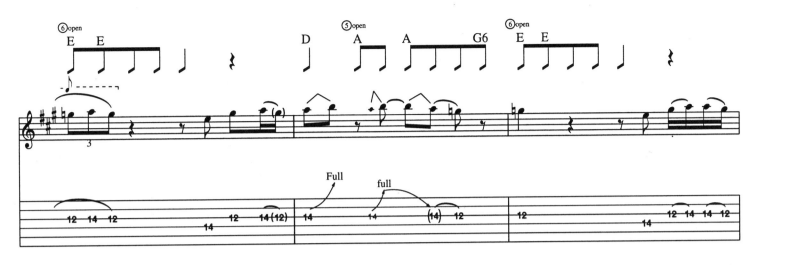

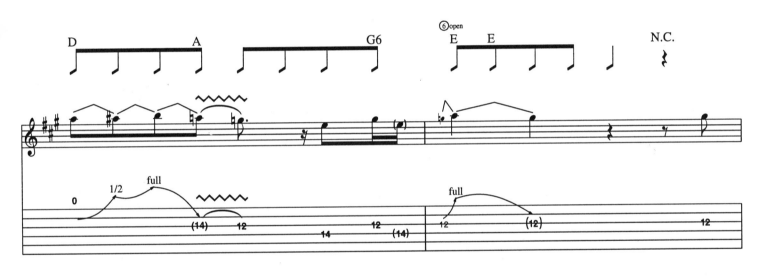

She Came In Through The Bathroom Window

Words and Music by John Lennon and Paul McCartney

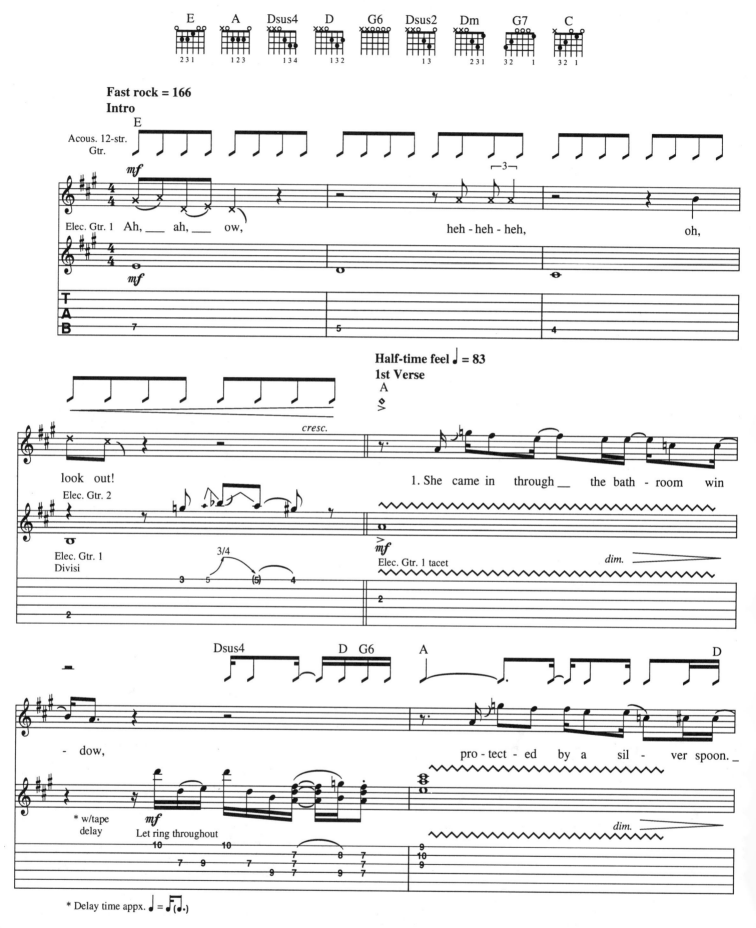

MCA music publishing

She worked at fif - teen clubs a day, _____

and though she thought _ she knew _ the an - swer, well, I knew _

what I could _ not say. _____   3. And so I quit _ the p'lice _ de - part

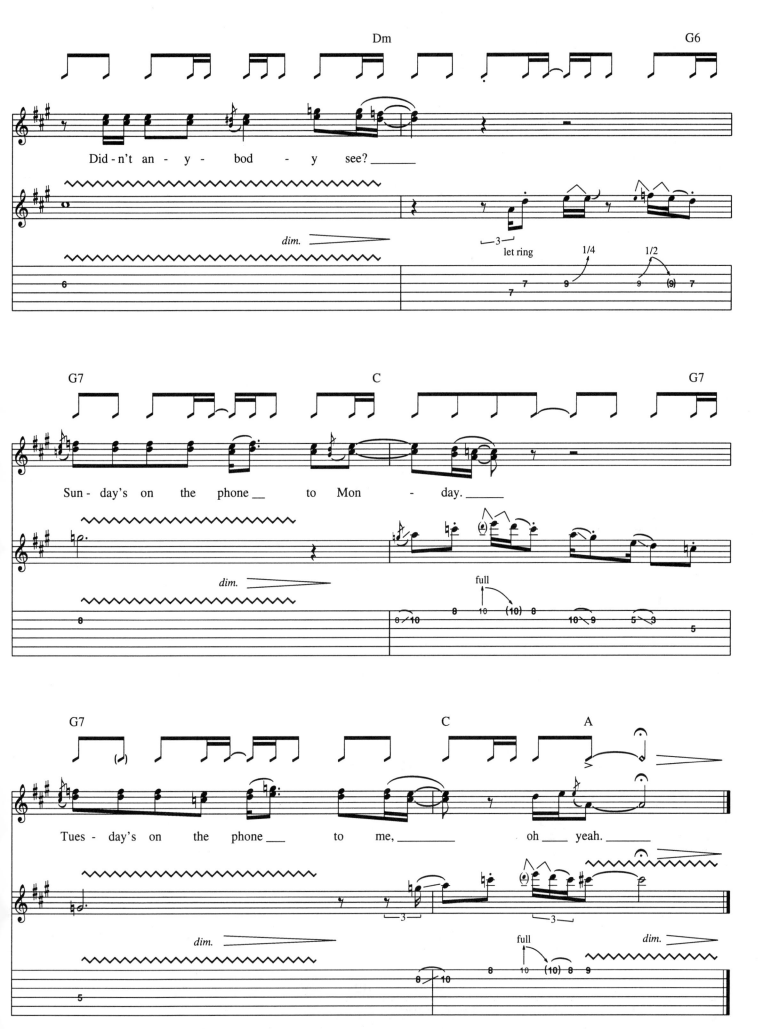

Golden Slumbers

Words and Music by John Lennon and Paul McCartney

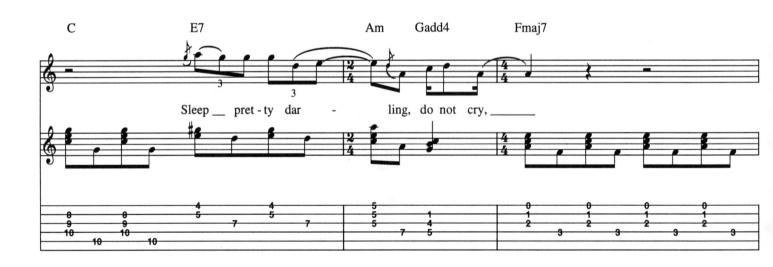

MCA music publishing

Carry That Weight

Words and Music by
John Lennon and Paul McCartney

MCA music publishing

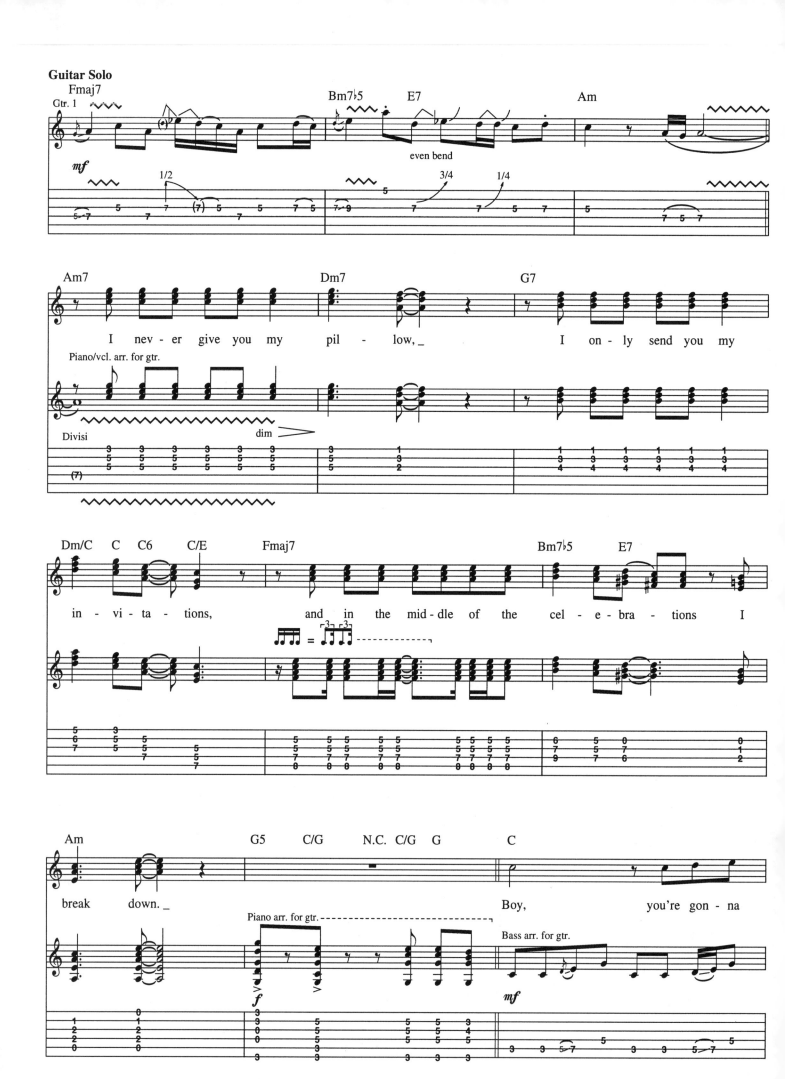

The End

Words and Music by
John Lennon and Paul McCartney

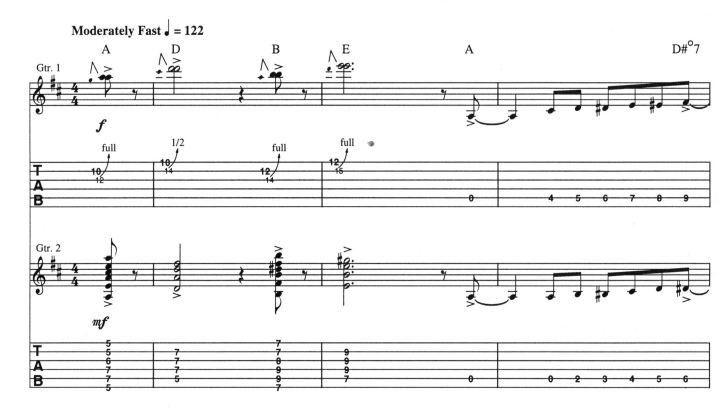

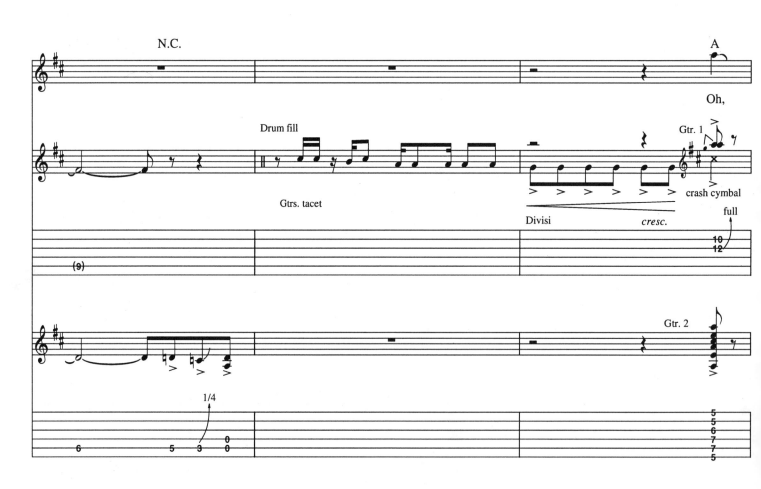

MCA music publishing

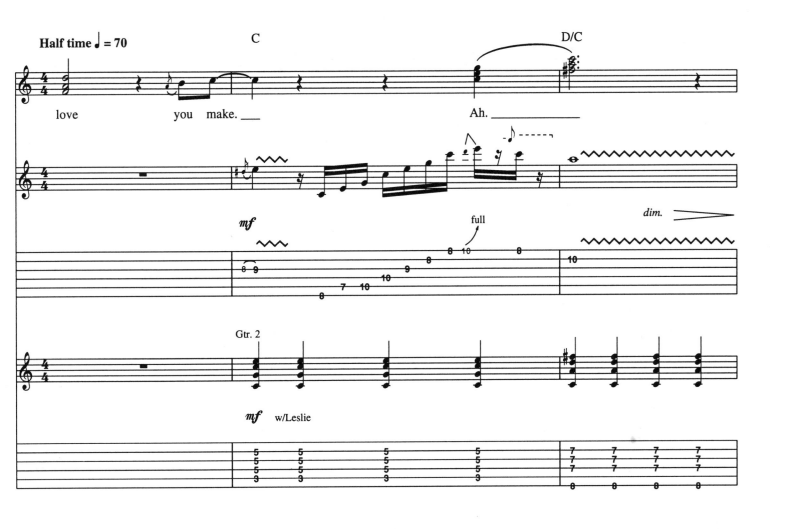

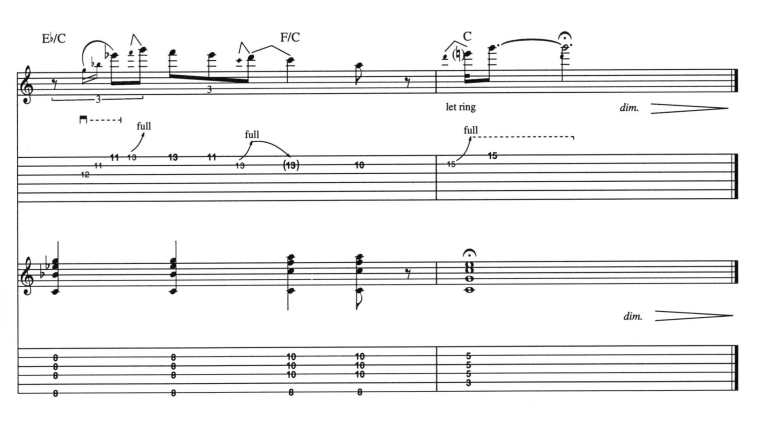

Her Majesty

Words and Music by
John Lennon and Paul McCartney

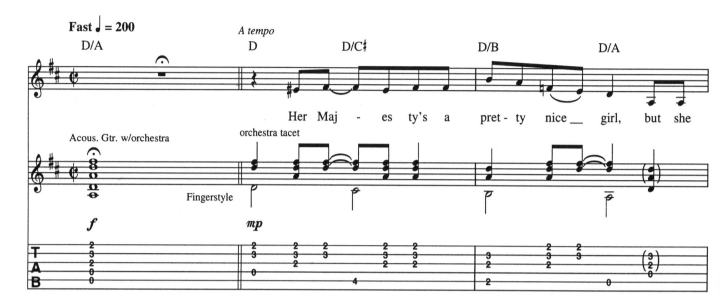

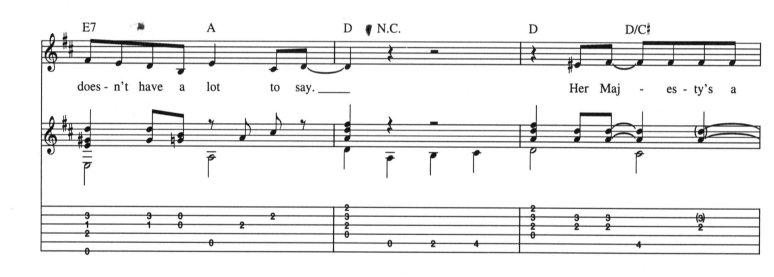

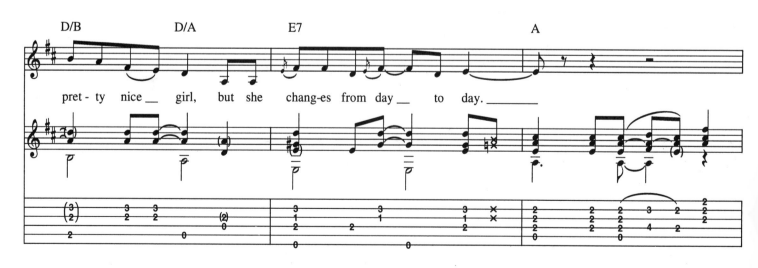

MCA music publishing

I wan-na tell her that I love her a lot, but I got-ta get a bel-ly full of

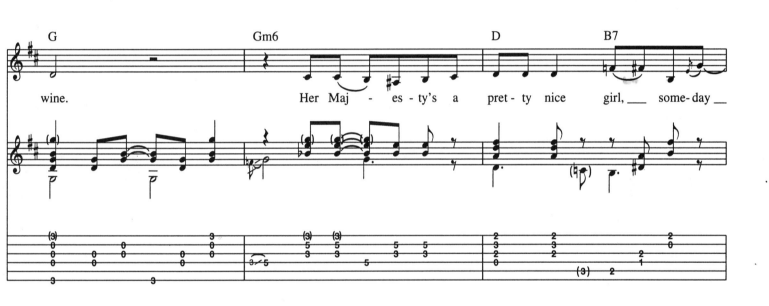

wine. Her Maj - es-ty's a pret - ty nice girl, ___ some-day ___

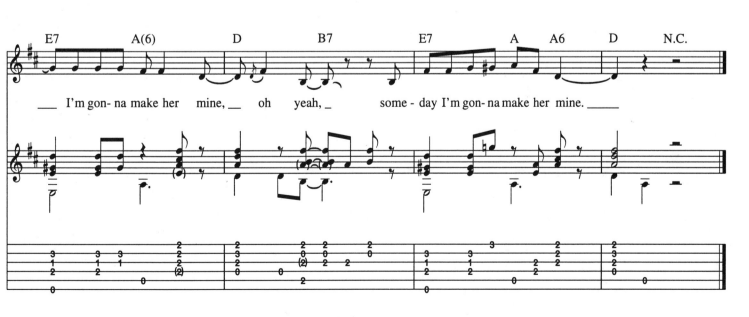

___ I'm gon-na make her mine, ___ oh yeah, ___ some - day I'm gon-na make her mine. _____

NOTATION LEGEND

RECORDED VERSIONS
THE BEST NOTE-FOR-NOTE TRANSCRIPTIONS AVAILABLE !

All Guitar and Bass Books Include Tablature

RECORDED VERSIONS FOR GUITAR

00692015	Aerosmith's Greatest Hits	$18.95
00660133	Aerosmith – Pump	$18.95
00660225	Alice In Chains – Facelift	$18.95
00694826	Anthrax – Attack Of The Killer B's	$18.95
00660227	Anthrax – Persistence Of Time	$18.95
00694797	Armored Saint – Symbol Of Salvation	$18.95
00660051	Badlands	$18.95
00694863	Beatles – Sgt. Pepper's Lonely Hearts Club Band	$18.95
00694832	Beatles – Acoustic Guitar Book	$16.95
00660140	The Beatles Guitar Book	$18.95
00699041	The Best of George Benson	$18.95
00692385	Chuck Berry	$18.95
00692200	Black Sabbath – We Sold Our Soul For Rock 'N' Roll	$18.95
00694770	Jon Bon Jovi – Blaze Of Glory	$18.95
00694774	Bon Jovi – New Jersey	$18.95
00694775	Bon Jovi – Slippery When Wet	$18.95
00694762	Cinderella – Heartbreak Station	$18.95
00692376	Cinderella – Long Cold Winter	$18.95
00692375	Cinderella – Night Songs	$18.95
00694869	Eric Clapton – Unplugged	$18.95
00692392	Eric Clapton – Crossroads Vol. 1	$22.95
00692393	Eric Clapton – Crossroads Vol. 2	$22.95
00692394	Eric Clapton – Crossroads Vol. 3	$22.95
00660139	Eric Clapton – Journeyman	$18.95
00692391	The Best of Eric Clapton	$18.95
00694873	Eric Clapton – Time Pieces	$24.95
00694788	Classic Rock	$17.95
00694793	Classic Rock Instrumentals	$16.95
00694862	Contemporary Country Guitar	$17.95
00660127	Alice Cooper – Trash	$18.95
00694840	Cream – Disraeli Gears	$14.95
00694844	Def Leppard – Adrenalize	$18.95
00692440	Def Leppard – High 'N' Dry/Pyromania	$18.95
00692430	Def Leppard – Hysteria	$18.95
00660186	Alex De Grassi Guitar Collection	$16.95
00694831	Derek And The Dominos – Layla & Other Assorted Love Songs	$19.95
00692240	Bo Diddley Guitar Solos	$18.95
00660175	Dio – Lock Up The Wolves	$18.95
00660178	Willie Dixon	$24.95
00694800	FireHouse	$18.95
00660184	Lita Ford – Stiletto	$18.95
00694807	Danny Gatton – 88 Elmira St.	$17.95
00694848	Genuine Rockabilly Guitar Hits	$19.95
00694798	George Harrison Anthology	$19.95
00660326	Guitar Heroes	$17.95
00694780	Guitar School Classics	$17.95
00694768	Guitar School Greatest Hits	$17.95
00660325	The Harder Edge	$17.95
00692930	Jimi Hendrix-Are You Experienced?	$19.95
00692931	Jimi Hendrix-Axis: Bold As Love	$19.95
00660192	The Jimi Hendrix Concerts	$24.95
00692932	Jimi Hendrix-Electric Ladyland	$24.95
00660099	Jimi Hendrix-Radio One	$24.95
00660024	Jimi Hendrix-Variations On A Theme: Red House	$18.95
00660029	Buddy Holly	$18.95
00660200	John Lee Hooker – The Healer	$18.95
00660169	John Lee Hooker – A Blues Legend	$17.95
00694850	Iron Maiden – Fear Of The Dark	$19.95
00694761	Iron Maiden – No Prayer For The Dying	$18.95
00693097	Iron Maiden – Seventh Son Of A Seventh Son	$18.95
00693096	Iron Maiden – Power Slave/Somewhere In Time	$19.95
00693095	Iron Maiden	$22.95
00694833	Billy Joel For Guitar	$18.95
00660147	Eric Johnson Guitar Transcriptions	$18.95
00694799	Robert Johnson – At The Crossroads	$19.95

00660226	Judas Priest – Painkiller	$18.95
00693185	Judas Priest – Vintage Hits	$18.95
00693186	Judas Priest – Metal Cuts	$18.95
00693187	Judas Priest – Ram It Down	$18.95
00694764	Kentucky Headhunters – Pickin' On Nashville	$18.95
00694795	Kentucky Headhunters – Electric Barnyard	$18.95
00660050	B. B. King	$18.95
00660068	Kix – Blow My Fuse	$18.95
00694806	L.A. Guns – Hollywood Vampires	$18.95
00694794	Best Of Los Lobos	$18.95
00660199	The Lynch Mob – Wicked Sensation	$18.95
00693412	Lynyrd Skynyrd	$18.95
00660174	Yngwie Malmsteen – Eclipse	$18.95
00694845	Yngwie Malmsteen – Fire And Ice	$18.95
00694756	Yngwie Malmsteen – Marching Out	$18.95
00694755	Yngwie Malmsteen's Rising Force	$18.95
00660001	Yngwie Malmsteen Rising Force – Odyssey	$18.95
00694757	Yngwie Malmsteen – Trilogy	$18.95
00692880	Metal Madness	$17.95
00694792	Metal Church – The Human Factor	$18.95
00660229	Monster Metal Ballads	$19.95
00694802	Gary Moore – Still Got The Blues	$18.95
00694872	Vinnie Moore – Meltdown	$18.95
00693495	Vinnie Moore – Time Odyssey	$18.95
00694830	Ozzy Osbourne – No More Tears	$18.95
00694855	Pearl Jam – Ten	$18.95
00693800	Pink Floyd – Early Classics	$18.95
00660188	Poison – Flesh & Blood	$18.95
00693866	Poison – Open Up & Say....AHH	$18.95
00693865	Poison – Look What The Cat Dragged In	$18.95
00693864	The Best of Police	$18.95
00692535	Elvis Presley	$18.95
00693910	Ratt – Invasion of Your Privacy	$18.95
00693911	Ratt – Out Of The Cellar	$18.95
00660060	Robbie Robertson	$18.95
00694760	Rock Classics	$17.95
00693474	Rock Superstars	$17.95
00694836	Richie Sambora – Stranger In This Town	$18.95
00694805	Scorpions – Crazy World	$18.95
00694796	Steelheart	$18.95
00694180	Stryper – In God We Trust	$18.95
00694824	Best Of James Taylor	$14.95
00694846	Testament – The Ritual	$18.95
00660084	Testament – Practice What You Preach	$18.95
00694765	Testament – Souls Of Black	$18.95
00694767	Trixter	$18.95
00694410	The Best of U2	$18.95
00694411	U2 – The Joshua Tree	$18.95
00660137	Steve Vai – Passion & Warfare	$24.95
00660136	Stevie Ray Vaughan – In Step	$18.95
00660058	Stevie Ray Vaughan – Lightnin' Blues 1983 – 1987	$22.95
00694835	Stevie Ray Vaughan – The Sky Is Crying	$18.95
00694776	Vaughan Brothers – Family Style	$18.95
00660196	Vixen – Rev It Up	$18.95
00660054	W.A.S.P. – The Headless Children	$18.95
00694787	Warrant – Dirty Rotten Filthy Stinking Rich	$18.95
00694781	Warrant – Cherry Pie	$18.95
00694786	Winger	$18.95
00694782	Winger – In The Heart Of The Young	$18.95

EASY RECORDED VERSIONS FOR GUITAR

00660159	The Best Of Aerosmith	$14.95
00660134	Aerosmith – Pump	$14.95
00694785	Beatles Best	$14.95
00660117	Black Sabbath – We Sold Our Soul For Rock 'N' Roll	$12.95
00660094	The Best of Eric Clapton	$14.95
00699331	Early Rock Hits	$12.95
00660097	Jimi Hendrix – Are You Experienced?	$12.95
00660195	Jimi Hendrix – Axis: Bold As Love	$12.95
00660201	Jimi Hendrix – Electric Ladyland	$12.95
00660122	Lynyrd Skynyrd	$14.95
00660173	Pink Floyd- Dark Side of the Moon	$14.95
00660118	Pink Floyd – Early Classics	$12.95
00660206	The Best Of The Police	$14.95
00699332	Rock And Roll Classics	$12.95
00660107	Rock Superstars	$12.95
00660096	The Best of U2	$14.95
00694839	Unplugged – Acoustic Rock Guitar Hits	$12.95
00694784	Vaughan Brothers – Family Style	$14.95

BASS RECORDED VERSIONS

00660135	Aerosmith – Pump	$14.95
00660103	Beatles Bass Book	$14.95
00694803	Best Bass Rock Hits	$12.95
00660116	Black Sabbath – We Sold Our Soul For Rock 'N' Roll	$14.95
00694771	Jon Bon Jovi – Blaze Of Glory	$12.95
00694773	Bon Jovi – New Jersey	$14.95
00694772	Bon Jovi – Slippery When Wet	$12.95
00660187	The Best Of Eric Clapton	$14.95
00692878	Heavy Metal Bass Licks	$14.95
00660132	The Buddy Holly Bass Book	$12.95
00660130	Iron Maiden – Powerslave/Somewhere In Time	$17.95
00660106	Judas Priest – Metal Cuts	$17.95
00694758	Lynch Mob – Wicked Sensation	$16.95
00660121	Lynyrd Skynyrd Bass Book	$14.95
00660082	Yngwie Malmsteen's Rising Force	$9.95
00660119	Pink Floyd – Early Classics	$14.95
00660172	Pink Floyd – Dark Side Of The Moon	$14.95
00660207	The Best of the Police	$14.95
00660085	Rockabilly Bass Book	$14.95
00694783	Best Of U2	$18.95
00694777	Stevie Ray Vaughan – In Step	$14.95
00694778	Stevie Ray Vaughan – Lightnin' Blues 1983 – 1987	$19.95
00694779	Vaughan Brothers – Family Style	$16.95
00694763	Warrant – Dirty Rotten Filthy Stinking Rich/ Cherry Pie	$16.95
00694766	Winger – Winger/In The Heart Of The Young	$16.95

DRUM RECORDED VERSIONS

00694790	Best Of Bon Jovi	$12.95
00660181	Bonham – Disregard Of Timekeeping	$14.95
06621752	Classic Rock	$12.95
00694820	Best Of Lynyrd Skynyrd	$14.95
06621751	Power Rock	$12.95
06621749	Winger – Winger/In The Heart Of The Young	$14.95

KEYBOARD RECORDED VERSIONS

00694827	Beatles Keyboard Book	$17.95
00694828	Billy Joel Keyboard Book	$17.95
00694829	Elton John Keyboard Book	$19.95